PRIVATE ROOMS

A One Act Comedy
in the Viennese Style

by
J. B. PRIESTLEY

LONDON
SAMUEL FRENCH LIMITED

Copyright © 1953 by J.B. Priestley
All Rights Reserved

PRIVATE ROOMS is fully protected under the copyright laws of the British Commonwealth, including Canada, the United States of America, and all other countries of the Copyright Union. All rights, including professional and amateur stage productions, recitation, lecturing, public reading, motion picture, radio broadcasting, television and the rights of translation into foreign languages are strictly reserved.

ISBN 978-0-573-11653-7

www.samuelfrench.co.uk
www.samuelfrench.com

For Amateur Production Enquiries

United Kingdom and World
excluding north america

plays@samuelfrench.co.uk
020 7255 4302/01

Each title is subject to availability from Samuel French, depending upon country of performance.

CAUTION: Professional and amateur producers are hereby warned that *PRIVATE ROOMS* is subject to a licensing fee. Publication of this play does not imply availability for performance. Both amateurs and professionals considering a production are strongly advised to apply to the appropriate agent before starting rehearsals, advertising, or booking a theatre. A licensing fee must be paid whether the title is presented for charity or gain and whether or not admission is charged.

The Professional Rights in this play are controlled by United Agents LLP, 12-26 Lexington St, Soho, London W1F 0LE.

No one shall make any changes in this title for the purpose of production. No part of this book may be reproduced, stored in a retrieval system, or transmitted in any form, by any means, now known or yet to be invented, including mechanical, electronic, photocopying, recording, videotaping, or otherwise, without the prior written permission of the publisher. No one shall upload this title, or part of this title, to any social media websites.

The right of J.B. Priestley to be identified as author of this work has been asserted in accordance with Section 77 of the Copyright, Designs and Patents Act 1988.

CHARACTERS

MAX, a famous actor, elderly

FLORIAN, a young poet

JULIA, a distinguished actress, middle-aged

ELSA, a young ballet dancer

A WAITER

The action takes place in two adjoining private rooms of a restaurant in a Central European capital

Time: about 1900

PRIVATE ROOMS

SCENE—*Two adjoining private rooms of a restaurant in a Central European capital, about 1900. Night.*

The stage is divided into two equal parts by the wall between the two rooms. Each has a door up C *near the dividing wall. The decoration of the rooms can be left to the producer and designer, who should, however, bear in mind the period and also aim at an effect of cosy intimacy. The dividing wall and the two doors must be solid and real, but the walls* R *and* L *can be suggested by dark curtains.*

In each room there is a supper table with a chair either side of it; if possible there should also be a settee in each room by the R *and* L *walls. The lighting must be warm and intimate, not spread evenly over each room but directed on to a tiny acting area in each case. It should be so contrived that it is possible to fade out the* LIGHTS *in one room quickly and at the same time bring up the* LIGHTS *in the other room.*

(*See the Ground Plan at the end of the play*)

When the CURTAIN *rises both rooms are lit, but preferably not too brightly. The tables in both rooms are laid for supper; and in both roughly the same stage of supper has been reached—the final stage of dessert wine and fruit, coffee and liqueurs. In the room* R MAX *is sitting* L *of the table and* ELSA *at* R *of it. He is a fine-looking man, of a theatrical type, who looks middle-aged but is actually elderly. He wears full evening dress.* ELSA *is a very pretty little thing, wearing a simple dress of the period. She is nibbling little cakes or fruit and taking occasional, rather nervous, sips of wine or liqueur.* MAX *is lighting a cigar with the air of a man who has supped well.*

In the room L JULIA *is sitting* R *of the table and* FLORIAN *at* L *of it. She is a very handsome middle-aged actress, wearing full evening dress of the period with plenty of jewellery.* FLORIAN *is an attractive young man in his twenties, shabbily dressed in the bohemian-artist style of the period. He is care-*

fully lighting Julia's cigarette; then he lights his own. No words are spoken for a minute or so but we should not feel they have been deliberately suppressed and that we are seeing a scene in dumbshow, but that the characters are naturally silent for a few moments, being full of food and drink.

The LIGHTS *fade on the room* L. *At the same time there is a discreet knocking on the door of the room* R *and the* WAITER *enters.*

MAX. Yes?
WAITER. Is there anything more you will be requiring, sir?
MAX (*glancing at the table*) No—nothing.
WAITER. Thank you, sir. Supper was satisfactory?
MAX (*considering this*) Um—yes—on the whole . .
ELSA (*bursting out*) It was *wonderful*.

(*The* WAITER *smiles and bows, then looks at Max*)

MAX. But you can tell your maître d'hôtel that I still think that the Steak Chateaubriand is better at the *Bristol*. There is something . . . However, I'll go into that another time. Nothing more now.
WAITER. Thank you, sir. Then you will not be disturbed again, sir.

(*The* WAITER *bows, smiles and exits. The* LIGHTS *fade in the room* R. *At the same time the* LIGHTS *come up on the room* L. *The* WAITER *is heard knocking at the door of the room* L, *then he enters*)

JULIA. No, I don't think there's anything else we want. You can leave us now.
WAITER. Thank you, madam. And supper was satisfactory?
JULIA. Most of it—yes. But I didn't ask for orange salad with the duck. You really ought to know by this time that I prefer prunes. I didn't want to make a fuss—I hate making a fuss—but please remember next time—no orange salad—prunes. That's all.
WAITER. Thank you, madam. You will not be disturbed again.

(*The* WAITER *bows, smiles and exits*)

JULIA. Don't you agree about the duck?
FLORIAN. If you say so—yes. But I hardly knew what I was eating.
JULIA. That's absurd. You must always know what you're eating. We have to eat so we might as well eat properly. Besides, why should I take the trouble to order a delicious supper for you, when I have so many important things to think about, if you don't appreciate it? Ungrateful boy! Aren't you ashamed of yourself?
FLORIAN (*smiling at her*) No—dear Julia—I'm not. A poet doesn't think of the menu when he's supping with a goddess.
JULIA (*smiling at him*) You're very sweet. (*She puts her hand over his on the table*)

(*The* LIGHTS *fade in the room* L. *At the same time the* LIGHTS *come up in the room* R)

ELSA (*enthusiastically*) I can still hardly believe it . . .
MAX (*smiling at her over his cigar*) Believe what, my dear child?
ELSA. That I'm actually sitting here with you—*you*! That this is a private room in our most famous restaurant, which all the girls are dying to visit, and that I've had supper—oh, such a wonderful supper—alone—with *you*. You can't imagine. It's like a dream.
MAX. The restaurant—the supper—or the man?
ELSA. I suppose in a way I can't separate them.
MAX. I wish you could. After all, any fool with a little money to spare could bring you here—give you supper.
ELSA. Oh—no—that wouldn't be the same at all. Naturally—I've had—invitations. Most of the girls get them. Oh—no, it's being here with you.
MAX. That's what I hoped, my dear.
ELSA (*in confidential, almost childish tones*) You see, I think it's through you that I fell in love with the Theatre. The first time I was ever allowed to go—for my parents were very strict—was to see you. We lived at Brinz, you know. You must remember coming to Brinz . . .

MAX (*vaguely*) Ah—yes, of course, Brinz. Place with the fine old market hall, isn't it?

ELSA (*surprised at this ignorance*) Oh—no. There's nothing special about the market hall. But the cathedral has a very very tall spire—quite famous—you must remember . . .

MAX (*who doesn't remember*) Of course. Stupid of me. Yes—yes—Brinz—with a very, very tall spire—and, as you say, quite famous. So you first saw me there. One night stand. What was I playing? The mad Emperor?

ELSA. Yes—the poor, mad Emperor. Of course it's ages ago . . .

MAX (*surprised*) Ages ago? Couldn't have been, my dear; I went out on that tour, playing the Emperor for one- and two-night stands, in all sorts of dreadful places, when I'd lost my lease of the old Duke's Theatre here and hadn't agreed to the terms of the Royal Company—and that's only six or seven years ago.

ELSA. It seems ages ago. I was at school . . .

MAX (*hastily*) Yes, yes, of course. Ages ago. But you remember the performance?

ELSA (*enthusiastically*) Everything about it. The wonderful acting—all the clapping and cheering—the speech you made at the end—the mayor presenting you with a laurel wreath . . .

MAX (*with a shudder*) Ah—those mayors and wreaths!

ELSA. Oh—did they do it in other places besides Brinz?

MAX. My dear child, I'd weeks and weeks of mayors and wreaths—to say nothing of the cabbage soup and slabs of veal with tomato sauce. Still, I mustn't grumble about provincial tours if one of them brought you into the theatre to see me.

ELSA. For weeks afterwards, every time I thought of that death scene, I began to cry. You were marvellous. I never thought acting could be like that.

MAX. Usually it isn't. But all this—as you say—was ages ago. Perhaps I've disappointed you since . . .

ELSA (*with fervour*) Never—never—never! You're still my favourite. Some of the girls say . . . (*She checks herself*)

MAX (*after a slight pause*) And what do some of the girls say?
ELSA (*rather confused*) Oh—they're just silly. I never take any notice of them. They think they know but they don't.
MAX (*quietly*) I think I know what they say, but thank you for not telling me—Lisa.
ELSA (*correcting him*) Elsa.
MAX (*hurriedly*) Of course—Elsa. (*He looks at her amorously, then takes her hand*) Dear sweet little Elsa!

(*It should be made clear* ELSA *does not want this sort of attention from him, so now she withdraws her hand from his and asks her questions hurriedly, to steer them both into safer waters*)

ELSA. Has a great actor a favourite rôle? I've often wondered what your favourite rôle is. Now you can tell me. Please tell me—tell me what you feel about all your rôles . . .
MAX (*accepting the diversion rather wryly*) I'd rather tell you what I'm feeling about you . . .
ELSA (*hurriedly*) No, no—about your rôles, please. Which is your favourite? The Emperor? Hamlet? Peer Gynt? That horrible Tartuffe?

(*As Elsa is speaking the* LIGHTS *fade out in the room* R. *At the same time the* LIGHTS *come up in the room* L. *During the following scene it should be made clear that* JULIA *is trying to get on physical terms with* FLORIAN *and not succeeding, although at this stage he is not deliberately avoiding contact but just not noticing the opportunities she discreetly offers. It is important, however, to avoid any suggestion of the farcical*)

JULIA. Your work, yes—it is good. The last play has some distinct possibilities. But it is you yourself who interest me. Just as I hope it is I, Julia, and not merely myself as leading lady of the Comedy Theatre, who interest you.
FLORIAN. Of course. Though I don't really see the difference—especially in your case.
JULIA. My dear boy, that's absurd. I'm a woman . . .

FLORIAN. If you weren't, you could hardly be leading lady of the Comedy Theatre. So what's the difference?

JULIA. I'm a person—not merely a performer . . .

FLORIAN. Yes, but on the stage you show us your charm, your wit, your intelligence, your depth of feeling, your beauty. They are all there for us to admire, to worship.

JULIA. So is the scenery. But I have a private life—I have a heart. What happens in the Theatre is important —of course. But what happens outside the Theatre is still more important. I may feel lonely—sad. I may need a devoted friend. So I say let us talk about each other, not about our work, dear Florian.

(JULIA *smiles at him and gives him a chance, which* FLORIAN *does not take, to seize her hand*)

FLORIAN. But my work is the best of me. That is why I want you to like my work before you like me.

JULIA (*tenderly*) Then you are too late. For already I like you very much indeed—you absurd, delicious boy. There!

(JULIA *gives another opportunity which is not taken. This time she is rather annoyed*)

Please give me another glass of wine. And take one yourself. Really, for a poet, you have drunk very little tonight.

FLORIAN (*as he helps them both to wine*) Then, according to my theory of creation and personality, if you like me so much, you must like my work even more.

JULIA (*dryly*) Unfortunately your theory of creation and personality may be nonsense. Indeed, it is.

FLORIAN. But surely, if an artist . . .

JULIA (*cutting in firmly*) No, Florian, my dear, I never discuss theories after supper. I don't even want to think of us as actress and poet—it is too late in the evening for us to be anything but our complete selves—you as a man, I as a woman. (*With a wistful smile*) Friends, I hope?

(JULIA *gives another opportunity, which is not taken*)

PRIVATE ROOMS

FLORIAN. Of course, though I have thought of myself as merely one of your innumerable admirers, a worshipper from afar, rather than as a friend.

JULIA. That is charming of you—very modest, too, much too modest. But at the same time, if I may say so, it does not show your usual insight and sensitive feeling . . .

FLORIAN. Oh—surely . . .

JULIA. Oh—I'm not blaming you. But now that I've shown you my true self, in all my womanly weakness, you should realize that it is not another admirer, even another worshipper, I need—but a friend.

(*This time* JULIA *offers her hand and* FLORIAN *is compelled to take it. But it is clear that his mind is elsewhere, and he soon relinquishes it. She frowns a little*)

FLORIAN. Then of course I'm proud to call myself your friend. This is one of the moments when dream and reality no longer contradict each other . . .

JULIA (*with a sigh*) Ah!

FLORIAN. Here are you—our greatest actress—and here am I—young—still almost unknown except to the discerning few . . . (*He breaks off and looks almost sharply at her*) But why did you say my last play has some distinct possibilities?

JULIA (*who does not want to discuss it*) Because it has. Accept my word for that. I know about plays.

FLORIAN. But is that all—distinct possibilities?

JULIA. You want to talk about the play?

FLORIAN (*surprised at the question*) But of course.

JULIA (*annoyed*) My dear man, it isn't "of course". Let me tell you something. This morning I read a play. At lunch I discussed a play with an agent. This afternoon I rehearsed a play. This evening, you may remember, I acted a play. And now, after supper, when I ought to be thinking about getting some sleep, you are surprised because I don't want to talk about yet another play.

FLORIAN (*plainly taken aback*) But I thought—that's why you had invited me here . . .

JULIA (*rather sharply*) I talk business during the day—not in private rooms at midnight. (*With obvious change of mood; laughingly*) Oh—stop pulling that face—and spoiling your handsome looks. Perhaps I invited you to have supper with me because your eyelashes curl and your nose is so intriguing and absurd. But what does it matter why we are here—so long as we are here? Really, sir, you're very ungallant. Here you are, in a discreet private room with Julia herself—where many famous men and rich men of this city long to be, I could show you their imploring letters—and all you do is to pull a long face because I won't tell you what is wrong with your second act . . .

FLORIAN (*embarrassed; stammering*) Oh—no—I assure you—I realize what an honour you've done me . . .

JULIA. Oh—stop talking that solemn rubbish! We are artists, you and I, and friends—we can talk out of our hearts. Smile at me. (*She leans across and deftly passes both her hands over his hair, caressingly. In a caressing tone*) Come—show that you forgive my stupid teasing. Kiss me!

(FLORIAN *kisses her, but awkwardly, without passion, briefly, and with obvious embarrassment.* JULIA *shows a touch of resentment but quickly hides it, regarding him mockingly*)

You're shy, aren't you, Florian?

FLORIAN. Not as a rule. But with you—yes, I suppose I am.

JULIA (*gaily*) Let us drink to our friendship!

(*She raises her glass and she smiles at him over it, while* FLORIAN *raises his. Then they drink*)

And now you must tell me all about yourself—so that you won't feel shy. Tell me about your father and mother and where you were born and where you went to school and—oh—everything. Come along now . . .

FLORIAN (*rather relieved at this turn of events*) Well—I was born and grew up in a very dull little provincial town called Brinz . . .

JULIA. Oh—I know Brinz. I've played in that draughty old theatre there—and nearly got pneumonia. When was I there last? Oh—years ago, of course. I think we were playing *The Lady From The Sea* . . .

(*The* LIGHTS *fade out on the room* L. *At the same time the* LIGHTS *come up in the room* R. MAX *has moved nearer to Elsa but is not actually touching her, though his arm is perhaps lying along the back of her chair. His manner should suggest that although he is not drunk he has had several brandies and is feeling the effect of them. His look and manner are definitely more amorous.* ELSA *is not yet alarmed but is feeling less confident than before, warned intuitively of his intentions. He is no longer smoking his cigar. We feel he has been already talking at length and is now becoming bored with it*)

MAX. So there you are, my dear. A question not of technique, as it is when you're still young and uncertain, but of mood. Not the mood of a moment, something that a kiss or a drink might cure, but the longer and deeper moods that reflect what is happening in the dark recesses of one's personality. Then, according to these moods, Hamlet might be the part one longs to play—or the Emperor, for into these rôles the actor, like the author before him, pours all those strange, hidden, dark feelings that suddenly rise to the surface like lava boiling up from an active volcano.

ELSA (*enthusiastically*) How wonderfully you talk! I think I could listen to you for ever.

MAX (*dryly*) I do these speeches very well, of course. Long training and experience must count for something. But the thoughts—even the actual words—are not mine. Most of that speech about the dark feelings came from some play or other, I forget what. So I owe it to some wretched author—some detestable fellow with a bad haircut, round shoulders, thick spectacles, and a squeak like a frightened mouse.

ELSA (*laughing*) All authors aren't like that.

MAX. Possibly not, but it's a fairly good generalized portrait.

ELSA. Do you really detest them?

MAX. Yes, my dear. We are dependent on them, and it is this dependence we hate, as most wives secretly hate the rich husbands who pamper them. That is why leading actors, who can do what they please, prefer to perform in classical plays—not because the plays are better, but because their authors are safely dead.

ELSA (*reflectively*) But many poets are young and handsome.

MAX. I doubt it. What is true is that many young and handsome men write verses, which pretty geese like you, my dear, mistake for poetry. Probably you know one?

ELSA (*rather confused*) Oh—no—not at all—I was thinking of Lord Byron and de Musset . .

MAX. Then I'll forgive you. But you should be thinking about me, here at your side . . .

(*Before she has time to resist* MAX *takes her hand and kisses it.* ELSA *does not shrink but is rather embarrassed*)

ELSA. Oh—but, of course, I am thinking about you. You have said so many wonderful things. I shall never forget tonight.

MAX (*fervently*) My dear, you are so young, so fresh, so innocent, so beautiful, that I listen to every simple polite statement you make as if it were coming from some mystic oracle.

ELSA (*humbly*) I'm sure I must seem very stupid to you, after all the brilliant clever people you know.

MAX. You don't seem stupid—you are enchanting. That is Point One. Point Two is that I don't know enormous numbers of what you call brilliant clever people. Point Three is that the few I do know I mostly dislike. Point Four is that it's time you came into my arms . . .

ELSA (*shrinking a little but trying to be gay*) Oh—no—I'm sure that's not Point Four. Now you're cheating—er . .

MAX (*prompting her*) Max. Go on—say it—Max . . .

ELSA (*trying it shyly*) Max.

MAX. Why do you find it so difficult to pronounce? Is it a name you dislike? Has it unpleasant associations for you?

ELSA (*rather embarrassed*) Oh—no. Only . . . (*She hesitates*)

MAX (*rather harshly*) Only what, then?

ELSA (*confused*) I suppose—it seems so strange—be-

PRIVATE ROOMS

cause you're so much—I mean, I have so much respect for you . . .

MAX (*who does not like this*) Respect! Respect! (*During the next speech he fills their glasses, hers with wine, his with brandy*) My dear little Elsa, there is no such word, no such attitude of mind, at such a time and in such a place as this. It is midnight in a private room, and you are a girl like a flower and I am a man who must recreate himself for the implacable challenge of tomorrow—and yet you stammer over my name and then babble about *respect*. Girl, either there is no true woman yet born in you or you are bent on eluding me. Have you a lover? Is there some infatuated oaf of a young man marching up and down the pavement outside, fighting his jealousy?

ELSA (*impulsively*) Oh—no—no. Nobody like that. Perhaps . . . (*She checks herself*)

MAX (*sharply*) Perhaps *what*?

ELSA. Perhaps I wish there was.

MAX (*not pleased*) Nonsense! They are ten a penny.

ELSA (*earnestly*) Of course that is how it must seem to you, looking down from a height. And also from there they must seem all alike. But I move amongst them, and although there are plenty of young men, certainly, and some of them would like to know me better than they do, they are not what I want—not the *One*.

MAX. There is no *One Man*. Don't delude yourself.

ELSA. The mind may not believe it but the heart must feel it. Or so it seems to me. So I must wait until my heart speaks.

MAX. It will never speak if you keep it on ice.

ELSA. But it isn't on ice. I feel it warm and alive, sometimes fluttering like a bird . . .

MAX (*leaning forward, staring into her eyes*) Is it fluttering now?

ELSA (*embarrassed*) It—feels something, yes . . .

MAX. Why?

ELSA. Because—well, I've admired you so long—and I'm proud that you noticed me among all the other girls in the ballet—and you've been so kind . . .

MAX (*harshly*) Kind? Kind? I am not kind. I am either

better than kind—or worse. (*He stares at her rather gloomily*) Now you don't understand what I'm talking about.

ELSA (*nervously*) No—I don't think I do . . .

MAX. Why should you? We talk too much.

(*Quickly, before* ELSA *can resist,* MAX *takes her face between his hands and kisses her, not too long and passionately, but very effectively. She releases herself and obviously shrinks from him*)

ELSA (*nervously*) Please—no—don't do that—please . . .

MAX (*harshly*) You find me repulsive? One touch repels you?

ELSA. No, it isn't that.

MAX. What is it then? You are afraid—of me, of yourself, of life? Tell me.

ELSA (*not actually rising, but preparing to*) It must be late, I think I ought to go now.

MAX (*urgently*) No, no, that will never do. You told me this morning that it didn't matter how late you returned to your lodgings, that you often sat up long after supper with the other girls. Now you say you must go because it must be late. That means you want to go, and that you want to go because I've offended you. Ask yourself where that leaves me—me, the man you pretend to admire so much . . .

ELSA. But I do, I do. It's true.

MAX (*not entirely without sincerity*) Then think of this. The night's still young and I hate to go to bed too early. But I am left alone because my guest, who was my admirer and, I hoped, my friend, has suddenly taken offence because of a harmless kiss—a girl, too, not straight out of some convent but of the Theatre, a colleague, a fellow artist, hurrying home because her lips have been touched. And here I'd be—alone—bewildered—saddened . . .

ELSA (*impulsively*) No—I don't want it to be like that—and it's not what you think—oh, it's so hard to explain—and, please, don't look like that . . .

MAX (*smiling*) Tell me how to look—and I will look it, so long as you stay to see . . .

ELSA. Well, just—sort of—friendly and relaxed—telling me about important things. Smoking a cigar—yes, that's it, smoking a cigar. (*She picks up a box of matches*) Look—here are some matches—I'll light your cigar for you . . .

MAX. I'm sorry—but I'm only allowed one cigar after supper. And what you really mean is—keep away from you—talk but don't touch. Very well. Observe. (*He ostentatiously leans back in his chair, regarding her mockingly*) And now I seem to see tears in your eyes. Why?

ELSA. If there are, it's because I feel you've changed. You don't really like me now.

MAX. Nonsense! Of course I do. And what I'm trying to do is to please you. But you must make up your mind, my dear. If I like you too much, you want to go home. If you feel I don't like you enough, your eyes fill with tears and your lip begins to tremble. You must admit that you make it very difficult for a man . . .

(*During this speech the* LIGHTS *begin to fade on the room* R. *At the same time the* LIGHTS *gradually come up on the room* L. JULIA *and* FLORIAN *are sitting as before, except that she is leaning forward, perhaps with her elbows on the table, and he is leaning back a little in his chair, smoking and looking rather sulky*)

JULIA (*as if ending a long speech*) And I say it's because you haven't lived. How can you write if you haven't lived? Tell me that. Don't just sit there looking sulky. Answer me. How can you write if you haven't lived?

FLORIAN. If I'm looking sulky, I'm sorry. I'm not feeling sulky.

JULIA. What are you feeling then?

FLORIAN. Too full of food.

JULIA (*protesting*) Really . . . !

FLORIAN. Please remember, I rarely have a large meal so late at night. So it makes me feel heavy.

JULIA (*annoyed*) Sleepy and bored, no doubt?

FLORIAN. No, just heavy. But sulky? Of course not. However, I apologize once again for giving you the impression . . .

PRIVATE ROOMS

JULIA (*cutting in*) No, not that pompous stuff—I can't bear it. Talk like a man, a poet—not like a Minister of Forests or the president of an insurance company. But all this proves my point—that you haven't lived. I order a nice little supper for you—and refuse half a dozen invitations to be elsewhere—and then when I complain that you don't answer my questions, when I'm talking about you and your work, too, you coolly tell me you've eaten too much. Now what is the use of a man trying to write for the Theatre, if he can't take supper with a leading actress without falling into a kind of stupor? Better go back to—where-is-it?—Brinz.

FLORIAN. I've sometimes thought of it.

JULIA. You must be mad. But there again—it's the same thing. You're afraid of life.

FLORIAN. Nothing of the kind. Life is everywhere—and always I'm experiencing it, observing it, recording it . . .

JULIA. Fiddle-de-dee!

FLORIAN (*sulkily*) Very well then—fiddle-de-dee!

JULIA. There you are again! I only said that because you were beginning to talk about yourself as if you were a meteorological office, with all your observing and recording. And you know very well what I mean when I say you haven't lived. A little provincial town, miles from anywhere—a provincial university—two or three years here, writing paragraphs for second-rate newspapers—dreary little affairs with chambermaids and governesses . . .

FLORIAN (*annoyed*) I've never had an affair with either a chambermaid or a governess . . .

JULIA. Very well then. You think you're in love with some bouncing provincial music teacher or soulful milliner's apprentice, who, before you know where you are or have done anything worth doing, will have presented you with three hungry brats and a sub-editorship on the *Brinz Gazette*.

FLORIAN. Wrong again, dear Julia—quite wrong.

JULIA. So I'm your dear Julia, am I?

FLORIAN. Do you object?

JULIA (*with a sudden change of mood; smiling at him*) Of course not. Otherwise you wouldn't be here. (*She takes his hands. Quietly and tenderly*) I'm very fond of you—surely you realize that? And all that I've been saying is intended to help you, to further your career, to establish your great talent . . .

FLORIAN (*eagerly*) You do think, then, that . . . ?

JULIA (*cutting in quickly*) Yes, of course. Would I take all this trouble if I didn't? But when I say that so far you haven't lived, I mean that you haven't known the heights and depths of love, all the subtleties and ecstasies of a wonderful personal relationship, not with some moony raw girl who knows nobody but with some woman who is both an artist and a figure in the great world—the world that you haven't yet penetrated, but could know through her.

(FLORIAN *tries to interrupt*)

No, don't let us begin arguing again, dear Florian. It's all so futile and absurd when *we're* here—our real selves waiting to discover each other. Kiss me!

(FLORIAN *kisses her, but more or less as he did before, clearly without enthusiasm.* JULIA *does her best, without making herself look foolish, to encourage him to continue and improve the dalliance, but then, when she sees that it is useless, she breaks away*)

A cigarette, please!

(FLORIAN *is about to give her one, when she checks him*)

No, first, I must have a drink. I'm quite abominably thirsty. My throat's tired, I think. Perhaps I've strained it again. What a nuisance! (*She drinks*)

(FLORIAN *waits with the cigarette and matches*)

FLORIAN. Perhaps you oughtn't to smoke.

JULIA (*rather snappish*) Perhaps I oughtn't. Perhaps I oughtn't to do a lot of things I do do. But then I never pretended to be careful and cautious. I give myself freely to the public—and to my friends . . .

FLORIAN. Of course. Still—I hate to suggest it—but if you're feeling like that, perhaps I'm keeping you up too late—and we ought to go . . .

JULIA. Certainly not. That shows how little you understand me. After a performance like tonight's—not my biggest but one of my most arduous rôles—it takes me hours and hours to unwind myself, to allow my heart to beat quietly again, to face the thought of being alone.

FLORIAN. Naturally. I've felt that myself—after seeing something of mine performed—when I've stood there acting everybody's part . . .

JULIA (*ignoring his speech*) So always at these times I must be with somebody who understands me, who loves me, who is ready to share my triumphs or to calm my fears. I *give* everything. I *want* everything—devotion, comradeship—and passion.

FLORIAN (*offering the cigarette*) The cigarette now?

JULIA. Yes, please.

(FLORIAN *lights it for her. Then she looks at him*)

Why do you think you have no passion?

FLORIAN (*rather taken aback*) I didn't know I did

JULIA. You do. It is what is chiefly wrong with your work. It lacks passion—or any understanding of it. Because you lack experience. Because you are too introspective. So you imagine you are cold—that no relation with a woman can move you to the depths, raise you to the heights. And why? Why, my friend?

FLORIAN. I don't agree with this. But tell me why.

JULIA. Because you have never known a woman. Girls, yes—but not a woman. You think it is something lacking in yourself. Nonsense! It is merely that up to now you have had no opportunity. It is your experience that is at fault. Correct that, and the result will show in your work at once. Now it is too dry and cold. It needs warmth, more life. And where are you to find them?

FLORIAN (*eagerly*) I don't agree that it needs more warmth, more life. Take my last play . . .

JULIA. My dear, we have been taking your last

PRIVATE ROOMS

play all night. Now let's talk about something more amusing . . .

(FLORIAN *jumps up in a rage.* JULIA *instantly changes her mood, seizing his coat sleeves and pulling him back into his chair*)

(*In a coaxing tone*) Don't be stupid, darling. You mustn't allow yourself to be teased into a rage like that. I'm famous for it—ask them at the Theatre. Look—you need another drink . . . (*She pours him a drink. Winningly*) I was thinking of you this afternoon at rehearsal because something ridiculous happened and I thought at once "I must remember to tell Florian that tonight. He'll adore it—with his lovely sense of humour." You see, we were running through the second act—and that old monster Fritz, who's really too fat to be seen in public any more, came waddling on . . .

(*During this speech the* LIGHTS *fade out on the room* L. *At the same time the* LIGHTS *come up on the room* R. MAX *is now standing up, glaring down at* ELSA *who is looking up at him imploringly*)

ELSA (*imploringly*) Please—please don't be angry—I think I can explain . . .

MAX (*relaxing a little*) Very well. Explain.

ELSA (*earnestly*) It's perfectly true I like you—I like you very much. And I've admired you, everything you've done—oh—for years and years . . .

MAX (*grimly*) But stopped ten minutes ago.

ELSA. Please sit down again—and listen . . .

MAX (*sitting; still grimly*) Go on. You've admired me for years and years—still do . . .

ELSA. Yes, of course. And I'm grateful—terribly grateful . . .

MAX. I'm honoured. But I haven't noticed any particular demonstration of gratitude . . .

ELSA. If you asked me to do anything for you—to cook for you—to clean out your room—to mend your clothes —I'd be glad and proud to do it.

MAX. So you say. I must point out, however, as you

must have already guessed, Miss Elsa, that I already have an excellent cook, my rooms are in no need of cleaning, and when my clothes have to be mended I give them away. So you cannot show your gratitude in those directions. As you know very well, you little humbug. But when I *do* ask you to do something—which costs little—you immediately refuse me . . .

ELSA (*distressed but firm*) Because what you want doesn't cost little—it costs everything. But that's not it. There's something in me that doesn't care how much I admire you, how grateful I am, how proud I am that I'm here with you, but simply won't let you touch me. I can't help it. I'm sorry. I tried to show you—so that you wouldn't try and then be angry .

MAX (*wearily*) Yes—yes—yes—yes. (*He buries his face in his hands for a moment*)

ELSA (*quieter now; with a touch of accusation*) You see, you don't really care at all about me now. You don't *love* me.

MAX (*staring at her*) Have I ever suggested I did?

ELSA. No. Otherwise it would have been harder still.

MAX. It would be like playing poker with marked cards. Even lecherous old rogues who lure high-minded young girls into private rooms may have their codes of honour . . .

ELSA. Don't talk about yourself like that. It hurts me as well as you. Not only what you say but—worse still—the way you're saying it . . .

MAX. Have I to have a lecture now—from one of the youngest members of the ballet?

ELSA (*almost breaking down*) Oh—please stop—it's horrible—horrible—you've spoilt everything—and I thought it would be so wonderful—being here with you.

MAX. Accept my apologies for the horror of the situation, although a great many women, some of them quite young, too, would disagree with your verdict.

ELSA (*with more spirit*) I can't believe that, though it's nothing to do with me. But don't you see that if it were just a man—any man—behaving stupidly, it wouldn't matter—I'd—I'd hit him and run away. It's because it's you—and now you're angry and feeling hurt—and yet I can't help it . . .

MAX (*coldly*) Don't be too sure you can't help it. In any event you seem to me, in spite of your admirable performance, something of a young hypocrite.

ELSA (*protesting*) No. No.

MAX. If I had asked you to see me in my room at the theatre, pretending it was theatrical business—a familiar gambit, but not one I use—then you would have some excuse to feel shocked. But I asked you to have supper with me in a private room of a restaurant. You must have known what that meant—that if I felt like it I would make love to you. It appears that this is distasteful to you. At close quarters apparently I am repulsive . .

ELSA. No—no, please—you mustn't see it like that . . .

MAX. Believe me, my dear girl, no man would choose to see it like that if he could find some other explanation. We seem to be most easily and yet most deeply wounded in our vanity as sexual animals. Absurd, monstrous, but true. I can feel the knife turning now. But having struck the blow, which as a woman you were entitled to do, you mustn't pretend to be shocked, horrified, disillusioned, by my behaviour—which incidentally has been well above the average behaviour of a host in this room. That is why I called you a young hypocrite. (*He begins to bend over her, ready to take her in his arms by force if necessary*) And in that character you don't excite my sympathy. I don't see why I shouldn't please myself as you have been pleasing yourself up to now, taking all and giving nothing. Now it seems to me it is my turn. You have had your supper—and now you must sing for it.

(*During the last part of this speech the* LIGHTS *fade on the room* R. *At the same time the* LIGHTS *come up in the room* L. *The position here now is that both* JULIA *and* FLORIAN, *for different reasons, are bored. Although the room* R *is now dark,* MAX *must seize* ELSA *in his arms and begin to overpower her in spite of her struggles; this must be done entirely without sound*)

JULIA (*not without malice*) That is another thing, of

course. You have no humour. It goes with the lack of warmth, of life.

FLORIAN. Quite wrong. It goes with the lack of shallowness, of cynicism. I don't pretend to have any humour. I don't need it, don't like it.

JULIA. You may not like it but you certainly need it, my dear boy. A lighter touch would make all the difference . . .

FLORIAN. Oh—that light touch! For years now we have had nothing but that light touch—the *boudoir* style, the millinery manner . . .

JULIA. It has its weaknesses, certainly. But it is better than undergraduate earnestness, the ferocity of provincial debating societies . . .

FLORIAN. An hour ago you were agreeing with me. I don't understand you . . .

JULIA. I'm delighted to hear it. Unfortunately I understand you only too well. Yours is the more interesting situation. (*She yawns ostentatiously*) Oh—I beg your pardon! I'm not usually so sleepy at this hour.

FLORIAN (*jumping up, angrily*) I'm sorry if I've bored you . . .

JULIA. Oh—come—come! I never said that. Once or twice, I thought, you were quite amusing . . .

(*A scream from* ELSA, *who is genuinely frightened, is heard from next door, not too loud but quite distinctly*)

FLORIAN (*alert*) Did you hear that?

JULIA. Yes. From the next room. No need to interfere . . .

FLORIAN. Yes, there is. (*He rushes to the door*)

JULIA (*rising*) Now don't make a fool of yourself, you stupid boy . . .

(FLORIAN *exits quickly from the room* L, *and bursts into the room* R.

As he does so the LIGHTS *fade out in the room* L. *At the same time the* LIGHTS *come up in the room* R)

FLORIAN (*as he enters*) What's happening? Can I help?

(MAX *and* ELSA *spring apart.* FLORIAN *and* ELSA *stare at each other in amazement*)

ELSA (*breathless*) You!
FLORIAN. You!
MAX (*coolly*) Very nicely timed. But, I imagine, well rehearsed, too. Um?
FLORIAN. Certainly not, sir. I was in the room next door. I heard this young lady scream—I thought, for help. So . . .
MAX (*cutting in*) You came to her rescue—and staged a fine little recognition scene. I've played dozens of 'em. (*Mimicking them*) You! *You!* (*Resuming his former cool, sceptical manner*) But are you sure you weren't hanging about in the corridor out there, waiting for the agreed signal?
FLORIAN (*indignantly*) I was having supper with a lady in the room next door . . .

(JULIA *enters through the open doorway*)

JULIA (*as she enters*) That's quite true. He was having supper with me . . . (*Recognizing Max*) Max!
MAX. Julia!

(JULIA *laughs uproariously while* MAX *looks rather annoyed and* FLORIAN *and* ELSA *exchange wondering and interested glances*)

JULIA (*still laughing*) Oh—Max—you incorrigible old rascal . . .
MAX (*severely*) Julia, behave yourself.
JULIA (*looking from Florian to Elsa*) Are introductions necessary—or are you two young people already acquainted?
ELSA (*hesitatingly*) Well—yes—that is .
FLORIAN. We both grew up in the same town—Brinz . . .
MAX (*with mock despair*) What—are we all back there again? Brinz!
JULIA. We needn't be, Max. Florian, take her into the

next room and talk to her about Brinz. You don't mind, Max?

MAX. My dear girl—if that means you'll keep me company for half an hour . . .

JULIA. It does. Now—off you go.

(ELSA *and* FLORIAN *begin to move up to the door*)

(*To Elsa; as she goes*) All right, dear, aren't you?

ELSA (*giving her a look and a tiny smile*) Yes—thank you. I should like—to talk to—Florian . . .

FLORIAN (*jovially*) This way—then.

(FLORIAN *and* ELSA *exit and then enter the room* L. *They move to the table and sit fairly close together*, ELSA *at* L *and* FLORIAN *at* R, *talking eagerly—but of course in dumb show. In the room* R, JULIA *sits* R *of the table*)

MAX (*now the host; sitting down*) Julia my dear, this is a delightful surprise. Have a little brandy?

JULIA (*demurely*) Thank you, Max. Just to keep you company.

(MAX *pours out brandy for both of them, and then lights a cigar during the following speeches*)

MAX (*nonchalantly*) By the way, the little scene here, though not to anybody's credit, was not quite as ugly as that scream might have suggested. The girl was in no real danger.

JULIA. I imagine that. But really, Max—at your age . . .

MAX. Yes, yes, my dear. It's humiliating, of course—deeply humiliating. The nonsense one has to talk and to listen to! The glaring falsity of the whole thing!

JULIA (*coolly; murmuring*) Yes, I can imagine that, too. But why should you think for a moment it's worth it?

MAX (*ruefully*) Now and again—not often, mind—the temptation's irresistible. I saw her this morning at a ballet rehearsal—we're borrowing some of the girls for our next production—and she looked at me—so wide-eyed, so overcome—she's an admirer of mine. Or *was*.

PRIVATE ROOMS

JULIA. No, Max darling, probably still is. We all are. Even I am, within reason.

MAX (*who now has his cigar alight*) Thank you, Julia my dear. Cosy this is, isn't it? Like old times.

JULIA. But I still don't understand why you should think it's worth it. Even if you succeeded, what would it be? An awkward inexperienced girl . . .

MAX. I know, I know. But there are some things you women, with your terrible realism, don't appreciate. You imagine it's a girl's body that is the attraction. But it isn't—it's a lost world of youth—life in bloom again. The trouble is, my dear, we fellows who live in our imagination are greedy. We demand all over again the cake we ate years ago. We want to taste in age, when at last we can appreciate them properly, the confections we gobbled so eagerly in our youth. We refuse to be the slaves of Time, which takes its revenge by making us look fools and satyrs. My dear, you can understand that?

JULIA. I think so, Max. We have to fight and conquer Time in our work. Yet the people who applaud us just for doing that would be the first to blame us for—well—this . . . (*She indicates the room, the scene that took place there*)

MAX. Exactly. I've always said—you're a girl with a good mind, Julia . . .

JULIA (*with a rather bitter little laugh*) Girl! Thank you, Max. I'm only about fifteen years younger than you . . .

MAX (*surprised*) Fifteen? I thought—ten . . .

JULIA (*firmly*) Fifteen.

MAX. Well—fifteen—ten—whatever age you are now —you'll always seem a girl to me, Julia . . .

JULIA. Which makes you a very comforting person to be with, Max darling.

MAX. By the way—*were* you giving that young man supper next door?

JULIA (*airily*) Yes. He's a poet. He's trying to write something for me. This was the only time I could find to discuss his work.

MAX. No doubt. Is it any good?

JULIA. Vaguely promising. Not much warmth, much

life, yet. Lacks humour too. I was telling him so when—er—you interrupted us . . .
MAX. Quite, quite. Well, perhaps this encounter might help.
JULIA (*with a shrug*) It might. I wonder what's happening in there?

> (*They both look speculatively at the wall dividing the two rooms.*
> *The* LIGHTS *fade out immediately on the room* R. *At the same time the* LIGHTS *come up on the room* L. FLORIAN *and* ELSA, *locked in each other's arms, are now sprawled across the settee*)

FLORIAN (*murmuring*) Darling!
ELSA (*murmuring ecstatically*) Darling—darling!

> (*The* LIGHTS *fade out on the room* L. *At the same time the* LIGHTS *come up in the room* R. JULIA *and* MAX *look at each other*)

MAX (*with a shrug and a smile*) Well, whatever's happening, I notice there aren't any more screams. And I must say, for all my talk about lost worlds and the bloom of youth and the rest of it . . .
JULIA. Yes, Max, and I seem to remember a speech rather like that in *The Awakening* . . .
MAX. Of course—*The Awakening*—I couldn't remember where I'd got it. But, as I was saying, for all my talk, it's a relief to be with—well, I won't say a contemporary—but—you know . . .
JULIA. Yes, I know. And I could almost say the same, though of course my supper party wasn't quite like yours . . .
MAX (*murmuring with a trace of irony*) Naturally . . .

> (JULIA *suddenly laughs reminiscently*)

Hello—what's this?
JULIA (*with animation*) I've just remembered something else. Do you know where it was that you and I—first . . . ?

MAX (*cutting into her hesitation*) No, as a matter of fact I've been trying to remember . . .

JULIA. You wicked old rascal! I oughtn't to tell you. But it was in that awful place . . . (*She points to the wall*)

MAX. Not Brinz?

JULIA (*laughing*) Yes—Brinz. Don't you remember—we were out with *Doll's House* and *Rosmersholm*—and I'd caught cold in that fiendish draughty old theatre—just at the wrong moment, of course; I was *furious*—and I wouldn't let you come near me—and then you mixed some terribly strong hot punch . . .

MAX (*eagerly*) You're right, my dear. And old Dorgenheim burst in on us—and by that time you were pickled . . .

JULIA (*laughing*) And so were you—worse than I was—and old Dorgenheim shouted and stormed at us—and swore he'd have us out of the company . . .

MAX (*laughing*) And I'd taken that old green cloak of his, you remember . . .

JULIA (*laughing*) And the fur hat he always wore in winter—you remember the fur hat, darling . . . ?

The CURTAIN *begins to fall*

MAX (*laughing*) And what was it he said—what was it . . . ?

But the CURTAIN *is now down*

FURNITURE AND PROPERTY PLOT

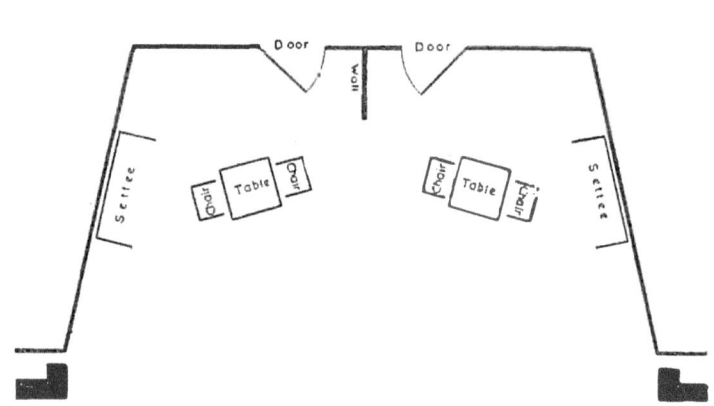

On stage: *In room* R: Table. *On it:* tablecloth, supper dessert dishes, etc., fruit, bottle of wine, bottle of brandy, wineglass, 2 brandy glasses, ashtray, matches
2 chairs
Settee

In room L: Table. *On it:* tablecloth, supper dessert dishes, etc., bottle of wine, ashtray, matches, 2 wineglasses
2 chairs
Settee

Personal: MAX: cigar case with cigars
FLORIAN: cigarette case with cigarettes

LIGHTING PLOT

Two private rooms in a restaurant
Interior. Night
THE MAIN ACTING AREAS in each room are round the tables (LC and RC), and by the doors (up C). A circle of light should light only this part of the stage in each case.

To open: Both rooms lit with warm, intimate light, not too bright

Cue 1   After pause at rise of CURTAIN   (page 2)
Fade out lights on room L

Cue 2   The WAITER exits   (page 2)
Fade out lights on room R
Bring up lights on room L

Cue 3   JULIA: You're very sweet.   (page 3)
Fade out lights on room L
Bring up lights on room R

Cue 4   ELSA: ... Peer Gynt? That horrible Tartuffe?   (page 5)
Fade out lights on room R
Bring up lights on room L

Cue 5   JULIA: ... I think we were playing *The Lady From The Sea.*   (page 8)
Fade out lights on room L
Bring up lights on room R

Cue 6   MAX: You must admit that you make it very difficult for a man   (page 13)
Fade out lights on room R
Bring up lights on room L

Cue 7   JULIA: ... came waddling on.   (page 17)
Fade out lights on room L
Bring up lights on room R

PRIVATE ROOMS

Cue 8   Max: . . . and now you must sing for it.   (page 19)
         Fade out lights on room R
         Bring up lights on room L

Cue 9   Florian exits   (page 20)
         Fade out lights on room L
         Bring up lights on room R

Cue 10 Julia: . . . I wonder what's happening in
         there   (page 24)
         Fade out lights on room R *quickly*
         Bring in lights on room L

Cue 11 Elsa: Darling—darling!   (page 24)
         Fade out lights on room L *quickly*
         Bring up lights on room R

www.ingramcontent.com/pod-product-compliance
Ingram Content Group UK Ltd.
Pitfield, Milton Keynes, MK11 3LW, UK
UKHW021848210426
5322IPUK00022B/546